Y0-CXM-447

How to

Edit & Revise

Your Essay

Step-by-Step

Step-by-Step Study Skills

Happy Frog Learning

Copyright 2021 by Jay Matthews

All rights reserved. This book or any portion thereof
may not be reproduced or used in any manner whatsoever
without the express written permission of the publisher
except for the use of brief quotations in a book review.

Table of Contents

Introduction

Welcome to **How to Edit & Revise Your Essay**. This book teaches you how to improve your essay by revising what you have already written.

Essay editing skills are important for all students. A quick edit can be the difference between an average grade and an excellent one. Moreover, editing skills benefit every subject with written assignments - English, socials studies, science, etc.

This book teaches you an easy three-step process for revising your writing. You'll see improvements immediately and become an editing expert in no time!

How the Book is Organized

This book is divided into three sections.

- Part 1 contains the **Level 1 checklist**.

  If you are new to editing, start with this checklist. The Level 1 checklist contains a high level of support as you learn the editing strategies.

- Part 2 is a **reference section** that contains explanations for each item in the editing checklist.

  When you first start, you may have questions about what a checklist item means. When this happens, flip to the reference pages for an explanation of what is required.

- Part 3 contains the **Level 2 editing checklist**.

  When you develop more confidence, you can switch to this checklist. The Level 2 checklist provides less support. It also contains several extra elements for you to review.

  Part 3 also contains a link to download PDF versions of the checklists.

Finding YOUR Editing Process

Essay revision consists of three steps.

1. First you check to make sure that you have a good essay **structure**. This means your essay is well-organized and contains all the required parts.

2. Once your essay structure has been strengthened, you revise to **improve the style**. This involves choosing strong over weak words, making sure you include transition phrases, etc.

3. Finally, your last check focuses on **mechanics** like spelling and grammar.

Once you complete the three steps for each paragraph, you are done!

Keep in mind, the editing checklists let you know **WHAT** you need to check. However, **HOW** you check is up to you.

Some people like to work through the checklist in order. They start at the first item and continuing step-by-step to the end. They review all the structure issues, then all the style issues, and then the mechanics.

Other people prefer to work a paragraph at a time. They review the structure, style and mechanics of that one paragraph before they move on.

Both approaches are effective. You might even prefer finding some combination that works better for you.

Experiment with the different approaches and find what works for YOU.

Good luck in becoming an editing expert!

Part 1

Level 1 Editing Checklist

In this section you will find the following checklists.

- Level 1 Structure Checklist
- Level 1 Style Checklist
- Level 1 Mechanics Checklist

The **Structure** checklist helps you makes sure that you have all the necessary parts of an essay.

The **Style** checklist helps you improve your word choices and sentence structure.

The **Mechanics** checklist finishes the revision process. It checks grammar, punctuation and spelling.

In the level 1 checklist, you are often asked to note down the details of your essay. This helps you decide whether you have met the checklist criteria, or not.

For the first few times you use the checklist, we encourage you to complete each step completely. When you are confident, switch to the Level 2 checklist at the back of the book.

Structure Checklist Level 1

Overall Structure   Page 19-23

☐ Essay has an introduction paragraph.

☐ Essay has 2 or more body paragraphs.

☐ Essay has a conclusion paragraph.

☐ Essay has a title.

What is it?_____

☐ Essay includes reference/citations.

Opening Paragraph   Page 24-28

Opening Sentence

☐ The first sentence contains a hook.

What is it?_____

☐ The hook is specific and does not contain vague words.

Thesis Statement

☐ The opening paragraph contains a strong thesis statement.

What is it?_____

☐ The thesis statement directly answers the essay question.

Linking Section

☐ The opening paragraph contains a sentence or transition phrase that links the hook to your claim.

Structure Checklist Level 1 cont.

Body Paragraphs   Page 29-34

❑   Each body paragraph contains a topic sentence.

❑   Each body paragraph contains details that support or exemplify the topic sentence.

❑   Each body paragraph contains a closing sentence.

❑   The closing sentence explains how the paragraph details support the essay claim.

Show the details for one paragraph:

Topic Sentence: _____

Supporting Details:

_____

_____

Closing Sentence: _____

Closing Paragraph   Page 35-37

❑   The conclusion (closing paragraph) repeats the claim but uses different words.

Write it here: _____

❑   The closing paragraph summarizes the main arguments.

❑   The conclusion paragraph leaves the reader with a final comment/thought.

Write it here: _____

Style Checklist Level 1

Weak Introductions   Page 38

❑   Avoid weak introductions like 'This essay is about', 'In this essay I will discuss', 'This paragraph tells you', etc.

Repeated Words & Phrases   Page 39

❑   Avoid repeating a word or phrase too often.

Vague Words   Page 40

❑   Replace vague words like 'big', 'small', etc, with more specific words.

❑   Where appropriate, replace non-specific words like 'thing,' 'it,' 'that', 'this', or 'there' with more specific words.

Weak Words   Page 42

❑   Replace common or weak words with more vivid words. For example, watch out for words like 'very', 'got', etc.

Sentence Variation   Page 43

❑   Make sure each paragraph has variation in the sentence structure.

Transitions   Page 45

❑   Include transitions between paragraphs to guide the reader.

❑   Include transitions between sentences when needed.

Style Checklist Level 1 cont.

Sentence Fragments
Page 47

❑ Fix any sentences fragments.

Informal Language
Page 48

❑ Remove any slang or idioms.

❑ Remove informal words and phrases.

Unclear Pronoun Referents
Page 49

❑ Make sure the referents/antecedents of all pronouns are easily identified. (i.e. Make sure it is clear who/what all pronouns are referring to.)

Mechanics Checklist Level 1

Capitalization & Punctuation   Page 53-54

- ❑ The title is capitalized.

- ❑ Names are capitalized.

- ❑ Numbers and dates are formatted correctly.

Fonts   Page 55

- ❑ The font is standard and non-distracting.

- ❑ The font is an appropriate size.

Spelling & Grammar   Page 55-56

- ❑ You checked for grammar issues.

- ❑ You checked spelling.

- ❑ You checked punctuation.

- ❑ Your lists have parallel structure.

Final Formatting   Page 57-59

- ❑ Name is in the header/footer.

- ❑ Each page is numbered.

- ❑ The file name is appropriate and spelled correctly.

- ❑ You met the word count guidelines for the assignment.

- ❑ You read your paper aloud to catch any final errors.

Part 2

Reference Guide

This section explains each item in the editing checklists.

If you need help for any checklist item, go to the listed page. The explanation will tell you what you need to do.

If you need more information about mechanics issues, a web search can often help.

If you need more information about structure or style issues, check out these books. They are available on Amazon or at HappyFrogLearning.com.

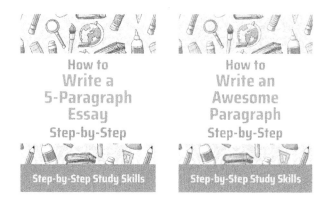

Essay Has an Introduction Paragraph

The **introduction paragraph** is the first paragraph in your essay.

The purpose of this paragraph is to:

- Tell your readers about the essay topic, and

- Give an idea of the information you will cover in the essay.

Make sure your essay has an introductory paragraph. Don't dive straight into the details.

Below is a short introduction paragraph as an example. From this paragraph we know:

- The **topic** of the essay,

- The **position** the writer is taking on the issue (also called a 'claim'), and

- A **summary of the arguments** that will be introduced to support the writer's position.

The position/claim and supporting reasons are also known as **a thesis statement**.

You can find out more about each of these parts in later pages of this reference section.

Sample Introduction Paragraph:

> In the US, junk food is consumed by about 85 million people each day. Even though it is extremely popular, junk food should be banned because it causes obesity, affects students' learning and can cause diabetes.

Essay Has Two or More Body Paragraphs

The **body paragraphs** are the main part of the essay. They come between the introduction paragraph and the conclusion paragraph.

A body paragraph provides information to support the claim you made in the introduction.

Below is an example of a body paragraph from a student's essay. This paragraph contains:

- A **topic sentence** that connects to the essay claim,

- **Evidence** that supports the topic sentence, and

- **Reasoning** that links the topic sentence statement back to the essay claim.

You can find out more about these paragraph parts in later reference pages.

Sample Body Paragraph:

> Another reason why home-cooked meals are better than restaurant meals is because of the cost. According to moneyunder30.com, you can save around $9 per meal by cooking at home. So, cooking just one meal at home a week, could save you $468 a year. Because of the cost, home-cooked meals are better than restaurant meals.

Essay Has a Conclusion Paragraph

The **conclusion paragraph** is the last paragraph in your essay.

The conclusion paragraph summarizes what you have written in your essay. Make sure you add a conclusion paragraph at the end of your essay. Don't just stop when you have written all your arguments or information.

The conclusion usually includes the **thesis statement** and some **final thoughts**.

Each of these parts is explained later in this book.

Here's an example of a closing paragraph from a student essay.

> To sum up, even though people enjoy eating out, home-cooked meals are better than restaurant meals. Home-cooked meals are healthier, cheaper, and helpful for people with allergies. So, next time you plan on eating out, consider eating in!

Essay Has a Title

The title is the heading at the top of your essay.

The title lets the reader know what the essay will be about.

To come up with a good title, consider using a reworded version of:

- The essay question from the teacher

- Your essay claim

For example, if your essay prompt is:

- Discuss the effects of technology on war.

Your title could be:

- The Effects of Technology on War

If your essay claim is:

- Cats are better than dogs.

Your title could be:

- Cats vs Dogs. Which are better?

- Cats are Better than Dogs

Essay Includes Reference List/Citations

A **reference list** is a section at the end of your essay that records all the books, articles, or internet resources you used in your essay.

The reference list lets the reader know where your information came from. Readers can check your references to learn more about what you said.

Reference lists usually follow a style guide. You can learn more about how to format your reference list in the Style checklist.

Here is a sample reference list from an essay about the pros and cons of being vegan.

References

"8 Nutrients You May Be Missing If You're Vegetarian or Vegan." The Healthy, 2021. https://www.thehealthy.com/nutrition/vitamin-deficiency-vegetarian-vegan/

Colon Cancer." Mayo Clinic, 2021. https://www.mayoclinic.org/diseases-conditions/colon-cancer/symptoms-causes/syc-20353669

"This Is How Many Vegans Are In The World Right Now (2021 Update)." WTVOX, 2021. https://wtvox.com/lifestyle/2019-the-world-of-vegan-but-how-many-vegans-are-in-the-world

Opening Paragraph:

First Sentence Contains a Hook

The hook is the very first sentence of your essay. It should be a statement of an interesting or fun fact related to your essay topic.

The purpose of the hook is to grab your reader's attention and give them a first idea of what your essay is about.

To find a good hook, try an internet search such as the following:

- Fun facts about ESSAY TOPIC

- Interesting facts about ESSAY TOPIC

If that doesn't reveal any interesting information, try searches with:

- WHERE/ WHY/ HOW MANY/ WHEN/ WHAT/ WHO + ESSAY TOPIC

Many hooks will work for your essay. Choose one that is interesting to you and **closely connected** to your essay topic. For example:

For an essay on endangered species:

There are over 16,000 species threatened with extinction in 2020.

For an essay on floods:

Flooding on the Mississippi River caused $6.2B in damage in 2019.

These facts grab your reader's attention and encourage them to keep reading.

Opening Paragraph:

The Hook is Specific, Not Vague

Where possible, your **hook should contain specific details** like numbers and dates, rather than vague words like 'big', 'a lot', etc.

A strong hook with specific facts will make readers want to read your essay. Vague words will bore your reader.

Carefully analyze your hook to see if you can make it more specific. Use the internet to find actual data rather than guesses.

For example, change:

> Many people die from smoking each year.

To:

> More than 480,000 people die from smoking each year in the U.S.

Opening Paragraph:

Essay Has a Strong Thesis Statement

A **thesis statement** is a sentence that states the main idea of your essay. It explains the position you are going to take on an issue**.** The thesis statement directly answers the essay question provided by your teacher.

Thesis statements are extremely important. **Make sure** you have a clear thesis statement.

Usually, a thesis statement consists of your **claim** (your position on the topic) and a summary of the **reasons** that support your claim. The thesis statement is usually the last sentence in the introductory paragraph.

Here's an example of a thesis statement that contains:

- A claim (ice-cream is the best dessert),

- And the reasons the writer makes the claim (because it is...)

    Ice-cream is the best dessert because it is delicious, easy-to-find and has many flavors.

As part of your editing process, check that your thesis statement contains a claim and supporting reasons.

If you don't have a thesis statement, your first step is to learn how to write one. You can find step-by-step instructions in either of the following books: **How to Write a 5-Paragraph Essay Step-by-Step**, or, **How to Write a Book Report**. These workbooks are available from Amazon.

Opening Paragraph:

Thesis Statement Answers the Essay Question

The thesis statement should **directly answer the essay prompt**.

The purpose of this check is to make sure you haven't gone off on a side-track and created an essay that is not on the topic the teacher asked for.

To check your thesis, read through your essay instructions, then compare it to your thesis statement. Does the thesis statement **directly** answer the essay prompt?

Example 1: Thesis statement is directly connected to essay question.

Essay Prompt: What is the best dessert?

Thesis statement: Ice-cream is the best dessert because it is delicious, easy-to-find and has many flavors.

Example 2: Thesis statement **is not** directly connected to the essay prompt.

Essay Prompt: Describe how the best dessert tastes.

Bad thesis statement: Ice-cream is the best dessert because it is delicious, easy-to-find and has many flavors.

Revised thesis statement: Ice-cream is the best dessert, and it tastes creamy, cold and delicious.

Opening Paragraph:

Transition Links Hook to Thesis Statement

Your introductory paragraph should contain a phrase or a sentence that **connects your hook to your thesis statement**. The link shows how your hook is relevant to your essay claim.

Here are some examples:

Hook	There are more than 2 billion websites on the internet.
Transition	Even though not all these sites are high-quality,
Thesis Statement	Children should be allowed to access the internet because the internet is educational, fun, and there are many online games families can play together.

Hook	66% of US children have internet access at home.
Transition	Although many parents worry about screen-time,
Thesis Statement	Children should be allowed to access the internet because the internet is educational, fun, and there are many online games families can play together.

Body Paragraph:

Contains a Topic Sentence

Each body paragraph should contain **a topic sentence**.

A topic sentence is a sentence that states the main idea of the paragraph. It tells what the entire paragraph will be about. It is usually the first or the second sentence in the paragraph.

In an essay, the topic sentence usually states one of the **reasons** that supports your essay claim. The remainder of the paragraph provides evidence to support that reason.

For example, if your essay has a thesis statement like the following:

Children should be allowed to access the internet because the internet is educational, fun, and there are many online games that families can play together.

Your first body paragraph topic sentences could be:

First, children should be allowed to access the internet because it is educational.

The remainder of the paragraph would provide evidence to support the claim that the internet is educational.

Body Paragraph:

Contains Supporting Details

Supporting details are facts, quotes or personal experiences that support or provide evidence for the topic sentence.

In an essay, supporting details provide evidence that the topic sentence is true.

Supporting details may start with 'For example.'

Here's an example.

> **Topic sentence**: The internet can be very educational.
>
> **Supporting Details**: For example, students can access a wide range of information to learn about any subject. In addition, students can go on virtual field trips without leaving their desk. Finally, online courses are available that can support any learning style.

Body Paragraph:

Contains a Closing Sentence

Each body paragraph should contain **a closing sentence**.

- The closing sentence is usually the last sentence in the paragraph.

- The closing sentence summarizes the main idea of the paragraph. It does not add any new details.

For example, in the following paragraph, the closing sentence does not provide any new facts about meerkats. Instead, it summarizes the previous facts as being 'interesting'.

Meerkats are small mammals that live in Africa. They live in family groups and sleep in a den. They are active during the day and share jobs like lookout and baby-sitter. Meerkats are very interesting animals.

Body Paragraph:

Closing Sentence Connects to the Essay Claim

The **closing sentence** of a body paragraph should connect the content of the paragraph back to the essay claim.

The simplest way to write a closing sentence that connects to the claim is to use a format like the following:

Because PARAGRAPH TOPIC, CLAIM

Here's a complete example.

Essay Claim: Children should be able to access the internet.

Body Paragraph:

   Topic sentence: The internet can be very educational.

   Supporting Details: For example, students can access a wide range of information resources to learn about any subject. In addition, students can go on virtual field trips without leaving their desk. Finally, online curriculums are available that can support any learning style.

   Closing sentence: Because the internet is educational, children should have access to it.

Body Paragraph:

Is Either a Supporting Paragraph or a Counterargument

Each of the body paragraphs should **either support your claim or be a counterargument**. The reader should be able to easily tell which type of paragraph they are reading.

Transition phrases are the easiest way to signal to a reader what type of paragraph they are about to read. Here are some transitions you can use.

Supporting Paragraph Transitions

- First, …
- Next, …
- Another reason…
- On the one hand, …

Counterargument Transitions

- However, …
- However, it can also be argued that…
- In contrast
- On the other hand, …
- In opposition to …

Body Paragraph:

Each Counterargument Gets Refuted

Each counterargument in your essay **must be rebutted (argued against).** You do this by providing additional evidence to show that this is not a strong reason to doubt your claim.

The research for your essay should have provided you with ideas for how to reject the counterargument. Usually, arguments are rebutted (argued against) in one of four ways:

- Accept the reasoning but **minimize its important** or significance.

- **Reject the claim** made in the counterargument by using evidence/reasoning.

- **Reject the evidence** provided by using evidence/reasoning.

- **Reject the reasoning** in how this claim counters your essay claim.

You can signal your opposing information with transition phrases such as:

- Even though …
- Despite …
- However, …
- Nevertheless, …

For example: in an essay that supports internet access for children, you might see the following counterargument and its rejection. (Using technique #1: acceptance and minimization.)

> Some people argue that the internet is bad for children because there is inappropriate information available on the web. However, while this is a serious concern, there is software available that can restrict children's access to inappropriate information. Hence, this is not a sufficient reason to restrict children from the web entirely.

Conclusion Paragraph:

Repeats Claim Using Different Words

The closing paragraph should **repeat your essay claim** as part of a summary of why your claim is true.

Do not repeat your claim word for word. Use different wording and an appropriate transition phrase. For example:

Original Essay Claim:

> Children should be able to access the internet.

Part of Conclusion:

> In conclusion, children should be allowed to access the many benefits of the internet.

Conclusion Paragraph:

Main Arguments Are Summarized

The closing paragraph should contain **a summary of the reasons** you used to support your essay claim. Any counterarguments should also be summarized.

The reasons should be summarized in one or two sentences. Try not to repeat your essay thesis statement word for word. Change it up a little.

For example:

> In conclusion, children should be allowed to access the many benefits of the internet. **As we have seen, the internet is fun, educational and families can play together. While it can be dangerous, this danger is easily handled**.

Conclusion Paragraph:
Ends with Final Comment/Thought

Close your essay **with a final thought** that stems from the arguments you have made in your essay.

There are several ways to add a final thought to your essay.

- Add a Future Thought
- Add Encouragement to Action
- Add a Question about the Content
- Add a Personal Opinion

Here are some examples how each of these strategies could be used in a sample paragraph.

> In conclusion, children should be allowed to access the many benefits of the internet. As we have seen, the internet is fun, educational and families can play together. While it can be dangerous, this danger is easily handled.

Future thought:

If we want our children to be good future citizens, we should not exclude them from our greatest information resource.

Encouragement to action:

Let's make sure all children have appropriate access to the wonderful benefits that the internet can provide.

Question about the content:

Is it really a good idea to limit such a wonderful resource when it can provide so much benefit?

Personal Opinion:

In summary, the internet should be available to children as long as it is limited appropriately.

Avoid Weak Introductions

Some phrases are recognized as being **weak ways to introduce an essay** or paragraph. Examples include:

- This essay is about..

- In this essay I will discuss...

- This paragraph summarizes...

Remove all examples of these types of phrases and rewrite the sentence so it is stronger.

For example, replace this example:

This essay is about how all schools should have uniforms because it is cheaper for parents, prevents clothing-based bullying and instills a sense of school community.

With this one:

Schools should have uniforms because it is cheaper for parents, prevents clothing-based bullying and instills a sense of school community.

Minimize Word/Phrase Repetition

When we write a first draft, we grab the first words that come to mind to explain our topic. When you reread your work, you might find that you have **repeated some words and phrases** too often.

It's best to replace repeated words so your writing is more interesting.

For example, replace:

John lit **the fire**. Next, he sat in front of **the fire** with a warm drink.

With:

John lit **the fire**. Next, he sat in front of **the warm flames** and read a book.

This recommendation is for 'content' words like nouns and verbs. Don't worry about how often you use 'function' words like 'the', 'a', etc.

Replace Vague Words - 1

As mentioned in the previous section, when we write a first draft, we grab the first words that come to mind to explain our topic. That's perfectly fine. But when it's time to edit, many of those words should be replaced with **stronger alternatives.**

One category of words that needs to be reviewed are 'vague' words. Vague words are words like 'big,' 'small,' 'tall,' etc. Your writing will improve if you replace these with more specific descriptions.

For example:

Replace: The cruise ship was really big.

With: The cruise ship stretched the length of the pier and into the bay.

Or: At 1100 feet long, the cruise ship stretched the length of the pier and into the bay.

Replace: John was tall.

With: John towered over the rest of his family.

Or: John towered over the rest of the basketball team.

Replace Vague Words - 2

Another category of words that should be reviewed are **vague words** like 'thing,' 'it,' 'there,' etc.

With each use of these words, make sure it is clear what you are referring to. If the antecedent (the thing you are referring to) is more than a sentence away, you may need to replace the vague word with something more specific.

For example:

Replace: John sat on **a bench** in the park. He hoped his friend would come soon. **It** wasn't very comfortable.

With: John sat on **a bench** in the park. He hoped his friend would come soon. **The metal bench** wasn't very comfortable.

Sometimes, deleting the words is the best option.

Replace: There were people sitting on the grass, reading books and listening to music.

With: People sat on the grass, reading books and listening to music.

Replace Weak Words

Another category of words that should be reviewed are **weak words** like 'very,' 'really,' 'got,' etc.

Use these words as a clue that you need to search for a stronger, more descriptive word. Your writing will improve immensely.

For example:

    Replace: John was **really hungry**.

    With: John was **famished**.

    Replace: John **got** a prize for his painting.

    With: John **received** a prize for his painting.

    Or: John **was awarded** a prize for his painting.

Vary Sentence Structure

In order to keep a reader's interest, your text needs to have **variation in the sentence structure**. Too many short or too many long sentences can make your text difficult or boring to read.

Compare:

> John was hungry. He made dinner. He carried his plate to the table. He dropped his plate. He watched the food splatter all over the floor. Oh, no.

To:

> John was hungry, so he made dinner. As he was carrying his plate to the table, he dropped it and food splattered all over the floor. Oh, no.

The first paragraph has no sentence variation. Each sentence is short and starts in the same way.

The second paragraph contains the same information as the first, yet it is more interesting to read. This is because the sentences vary in length and in their structure.

An easy way to check for variation, is to read the first 2-3 words of each sentence in a paragraph. If they sound similar, then it's time to add some variation.

For example, the first paragraph above would read: "John was. He made. He carried. He dropped. He watched. Oh, no." Can you see the similarity? All but one of the sentences are "subject-verb".

Let's compare that to the second paragraph. That would read: "John was. As he. Oh, no." Each of these beginnings is different from the others.

Include Sentence Structure Variation cont.

Now let's look at the sentence lengths in each paragraph. In the first paragraph, all the sentences are short, from two to seven words long.

The second paragraph has much more variation. The sentence lengths range from two words to nineteen words.

To sum up, to check for sentence variation:

- Look at the first 2-3 words in each sentence and made sure they have variation.

- Look at the length of each sentence and make sure you have both long and short sentences.

Now, how do you fix a problem with monotonous sentence structure?

You can:

- Add transitions to the sentence.

- Combine sentences.

- Or, if you have too many long sentences, break them into individual sentences.

Add Transitions

Transition words give signposts to the reader about where you are going next. This helps the reader and also makes your text more interesting.

For example, saying "first", lets your reader know you will be giving several pieces of information, or will be telling them several steps. When you say "second" or "next", you let your reader know they are getting the second piece of information.

Another example is the transition word "however." This lets the reader know that you may be about to say something opposite to what they might expect.

For example:

I like ice cream. However, pie is my favorite dessert.

On the next page, you will find a table of some easy-to-use transition words.

List of Transition Words

Beginning	First, To begin with, In the beginning, One example
Continue	Next, Also, After that, To continue, In addition, Furthermore, Another reason, Another example, Eventually
Alike	Similarly, Along the same lines, In comparison, Additionally, Likewise
Different	However, Although, On the other hand, In contrast
Result	As a result, Consequently, For these reasons, Therefore
Time	Suddenly, Occasionally, Frequently, When, Until
Example	For example, For instance, To illustrate
Quote	As X says, According to X, X states
Finish	In conclusion, In summary, Last, Finally, In the end, To sum up, In short

Correct Any Sentence Fragments

Sentence fragments are incomplete sentences. For example:

I need to buy a new sweater. Because this one is worn out.

The second sentence is not a complete sentence. It is a sentence fragment. You can usually tell something is a fragment if it doesn't make sense by itself.

You can correct sentence fragments by combining them with their 'missing half.' In the example above, the revised version would be:

I need to buy a new sweater because this one is worn out.

Sometimes you need to add the missing information. For example:

John decided to ride home on the old bike. Easy enough to do.

John decided to ride home on the old bike. He figured it was easy enough to do.

Replace Slang, Idioms & Informal Phrasing

Slang is a type of informal language, and includes words like 'cool' and expressions like 'check it out.'

Idioms are expressions like, 'It was a piece of cake' or 'pigs might fly'.

Informal words/phrases include words like 'kids' instead of 'children;

You should avoid using slang, idioms, and informal expressions in an essay. These words make your writing sound informal and less convincing.

Replace these expressions with more formal alternatives.

Check Pronoun Referents

For each **pronoun in your essay**, make sure it is clear who/what the pronoun refers to (the referent). Sometimes there can be more than one referent and the reader won't know which one you are referring to.

For example:

John met with Jenna's father even though he didn't like him.

Is it John who doesn't like the dad? Or does the dad not like John?

If you have a similar problem, rewrite the sentences to make it clear.

Even though John didn't like him, John met with Jenna's father.

John met with Jenna's father, even though John knew the man didn't like him.

Format References

A **reference list** is a section at the end of your essay that records all the books, articles, or internet resources you used in your essay.

References can be listed in different ways, depending on what **style guide** your teacher prefers (e.g. MLA, APA, or Chicago styles).

If your teacher has not introduced a style guide, use a consistent format like the following.

General Format for Books

Author-Last-Name, Author-First-Name. "Title". Publisher, Year.

Matthews, Jay. "How to Write an Awesome Essay Step-by-Step." Happy Frog Press, 2020.

General Format for Web Resources

Author-Last-Name, Author-First-Name. "Title of Article/Page/Video". Title of Website, Year. Website URL.

Dawson, Bethany. "Dinosaur Footprint Discovered on Welsh Beach by Four-Year-Old Girl." The Independent. 2021. https://www.independent.co.uk/news/uk/dinosaur-footprint-wales-discovery-girl-b1795156.html

If there is no author:

"Title of Article/Page/Video". Title of Website, Year. Website URL

"Citation Styles & Tools." Washington University Libraries, 2020. https://guides.lib.uw.edu/c.php?g=341448&p=4076094

Check Source Quality

Sources are the books, websites and videos where you found information for your essay. The sources you use in your essay should be appropriate – i.e each source should provide reliable and credible information that is relevant to your topic.

Keep in mind, the appropriateness of a resource can depend on the essay topic.

For example, an article on a celebrity news website might be perfect if your essay is about celebrities. However, that same source might be a poor choice if your essay is about nutritious eating.

To evaluate whether a source is high quality, ask the following questions.

- Is the article relevant to my topic?

- What are the author's qualifications?

- What is the author's affiliation?

- What is the author's purpose?

- Does the article/video contain opinion or facts?

- Who does this author quote: Are they quality references?

- How recent is the information in the article/video?

- Who is the publisher - Are they reliable?

- Does the appearance of the article/video provide clues to its quality?

Mechanics Reference Pages

In this section, you can find guidelines for grammar, punctuation, and formatting issues.

The suggestions here will work in any essay, but you should check if your teacher wants you to use a specific style guide. Style guides can differ in the rules they suggest for many of these elements.

Also, the information in this section is an overview. For more difficult situations you may need to consult a grammar book.

Capitalization

Capitalize the **first word** of a sentence.

- This is a sentence.

Capitalize **names** and other **proper nouns.**

- The story is about Mary who lives in London.

Capitalize the first word of a **dialogue quote.**

- She said, "Don't mess with the garden."

Don't capitalize the first word in a **word or phrase quote.**

- The dog was "crazy" during the night.

Capitalize **days, months, holidays, but not seasons**.

- I celebrate every Monday in summer.

Capitalize nouns, verbs, adjectives (and the first word) in a **title.**

- What Are the Pros and Cons of Being a Vegetarian ?

Numbers

Numbers can be written as words (five) or digits (5). Here are some general rules, based on the APA style guide.

General Rules

Use words for numbers from **zero to nine**.

- I bought nine cookies.

Use digits for numbers **ten or above**.

- I bought 15 cookies.

Exceptions

Use digits for numbers followed by a **unit of measurement.**

- The book was 7 cm wide.

Use words for any number that **starts a sentence**, unless is a year.

- Nineteen dogs howled at the moon.

- 2020 was an interesting year.

Use words for **common fractions and expressions.**

- I ate half the cake.

- July Fourth is my favorite holiday.

Use digits and the percent sign to write **percentages.**

- I saw 80% of the pictures.

Fonts, Spelling & Grammar

Fonts

Use a non-distracting font.

> **Good choice**: The third reason schools should be banned is….

> **Bad choice**: The third reason schools should be banned is….

Make sure the font is an appropriate size. Usually, 12 is a safe choice.

Spelling, Grammar & Punctuation

Make sure your essay has no grammar or punctuation errors. Use a grammar checker if possible. But please use your judgment as well. Grammar checkers and spell checkers sometimes make incorrect suggestions.

It's also a good idea to read your essay aloud. This will often alert you to grammar issues or awkward phrasing.

Check also for spelling errors. A spell check - along with your judgement - is the most effective option.

Parallel Structures

A parallel structure uses **the same pattern of words** to show that two or more ideas have the same level of importance.

Each element of the parallel structure must be in the same format.

For example:

- Martin likes **swimming**, **bowling** and **reading**.

- Tara like **to hike**, **to paint** and **to dance**.

- Some things you can do are:
    - **Get a lot of sleep**
    - **Eat healthily**
    - **Study hard**

Here are some **examples with errors**. In each example, one or more of the elements has a different format to the others.

- Martin like **swimming**, **bowling** and *to read*.

- Tara likes **to hike**, **to paint**, and *dancing*.

- Some things you can do are:
    - **Get a lot of sleep**
    - *Eating* **healthily**
    - *To* **study hard**

Check all your lists to make sure they have parallel structure.

Final Formatting

Title Page

If your essay is more than three or four pages, you might want to include a **title page.**

A title page is a single piece of paper that you put at the front of your essay. It includes your name, class, assignment title and due date. Here's an example.

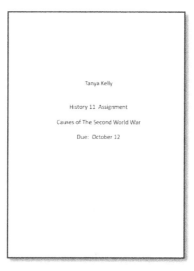

Tanya Kelly

History 11 Assignment
Causes of The Second World War
Due: October 12

Name/Class/Title is in the Header/Footer

Make sure your full name, class and essay title is on the essay. Usually, the best place for this is in the header or the footer, as well as on the title page, if you have one. Use your regular name, not a nickname.

Pages Numbers

Make sure each page is numbered. The title page, if there is one, is usually not numbered.

Final Formatting cont.

Appropriate File Name

If you are submitting an electronic file, make sure it is named appropriately. Ideally, you will include the following information in the file name.

- A reference to the class or assignment

- A reference to your name

For example, if Wen Lee is handing in the first assignment for a Biology class, an appropriate file name would be:

- WenLee_Biology1.pdf

- Biology1_Lee.pdf

The following filenames would not be a good choice as the teacher can't tell whose assignment it is.

- Bio1.pdf

- Assignment1.pdf

Word Count

Some assignments have a word count minimum you must reach, or a maximum you must not exceed. Check to ensure you are within any word count guidelines specified in the assignment.

Final Formatting cont.

Follow the Formatting Guidelines

Some teachers are very specific about the formatting of your essay. Check your essay instructions to make sure you have included everything required.

Read Your Essay Aloud

It is a great idea to read your paper aloud as one of the final editing steps. By reading aloud, you will find sentences which are awkward to read, or where you have used an incorrect word. You will find many more errors than if you read silently.

Make this step a part of your editing process.

Part 3

Level 2 Checklist

Once you are familiar with the editing process, switch to the Level 2 checklist. This checklist removes the extra supports found in the Level 1 checklist and contains a few more items to review in your essay.

Structure Checklist Level 2

Overall Structure Page 19-23

- ❏ Essay has an introduction paragraph.
- ❏ Essay has 2 or more body paragraphs.
- ❏ Essay has a conclusion paragraph.
- ❏ Essay has a title.
- ❏ Essay includes reference/citations.

Opening Paragraph Page 24-28

Opening Sentence

- ❏ The first sentence contains a hook.
- ❏ The hook is specific and does not contain vague words.

Thesis Statement

- ❏ The opening paragraph contains a strong thesis statement.
- ❏ The thesis statement directly answers the essay question.

Linking Section

- ❏ The opening paragraph contains a sentence or transition phrase that links the hook to your claim.

Body Paragraphs Page 29-34

- ❏ Each body paragraph contains a topic sentence.
- ❏ Each body paragraph contains details that support or exemplify the topic sentence.
- ❏ Each body paragraph contains a closing sentence.
- ❏ The closing sentence explains how the paragraph details support the essay claim.
- ❏ Each body paragraph either supports the essay claim (supporting paragraph) or is a counterargument.
- ❏ Each counterargument gets refuted with additional evidence/reasoning.

Structure Checklist Level 2 cont.

Closing Paragraph Page 35-37

- ❑ The conclusion (closing paragraph) repeats the claim but uses different words.
- ❑ The conclusion paragraph summarizes the evidence.
- ❑ The conclusion paragraph leaves the reader with a final comment/thought.

Style Checklist Level 2

Weak Introductions Page 38

- ❑ Avoid weak introductions.

Repeated Words & Phrases Page 39

- ❑ Avoid repeating a word or phrase too often.

Vague Words Page 40-41

- ❑ Replace vague words like 'big', 'small', etc, with more specific words.
- ❑ Where appropriate, replace non-specific words like 'thing,' 'it,' 'that', or 'there' with more specific words.

Weak Words Page 42

- ❑ Replace common or weak words with more vivid words. For example, watch out for words like 'very', 'got', etc.

Style Checklist Level 2 cont.

Variation Page 43

❑ Make sure each paragraph has variation in the sentence structure.

Transitions Page 45

❑ Include transitions between paragraphs to guide the reader.

❑ Include transitions between sentences when needed.

Sentence Fragments Page 47

❑ Fix any sentences fragments.

Informal Language Page 48

❑ Remove any slang or idioms.

❑ Remove informal phrasing.

Unclear Pronoun Referents Page 49

❑ Make sure the referents/antecedents of all pronouns are easily identified.

Reference List Page 50-51

❑ Each reference is formatted according to your chosen style guide.

❑ Each reference is a quality source that is appropriate for your essay.

Mechanics Checklist Level 2

Capitalization & Punctuation Page 53-54

❑ The title is capitalized.

❑ Names are capitalized.

❑ Numbers and dates are formatted correctly

Fonts Page 55

❑ You use a non-distracting font.

❑ The font is an appropriate size.

Spelling, Grammar & Punctuation Page 55-56

❑ You checked for grammar issues.

❑ You checked spelling.

❑ You checked punctuation.

❑ Your lists have parallel structure.

Final Formatting Page 57-59

❑ If appropriate, there is a title page with name, class, title & date.

❑ Name/Class/title is in the header/footer.

❑ Each page is numbered.

❑ The file name is appropriate and spelled correctly.

❑ You met the word count guidelines for the assignment.

❑ You followed the formatting guidelines for this assignment.

❑ You read your paper aloud to catch any final errors.

PDF Downloads

You can download PDF versions of the checklists for printing.

Level 1 Checklist: https://happyfroglearning.com/product/level-1-checklist/

Level 2 Checklist: https://happyfroglearning.com/product/level-2-checklist/

These checklists are copyrighted and are for your personal use only. The PDFs and links to the PDFs are not to be shared.

Congratulations on Becoming an Editing Expert!

Check out the other titles in our Step-by-Step Study Skills series to build your skills even more.

How to
**Write a
5-Paragraph
Essay**
Step-by-Step

Step-by-Step Study Skills

How to
**Write an
Awesome
Paragraph**
Step-by-Step

Step-by-Step Study Skills

How to
**Plan & Complete
School
Assignments**
Step-by-Step

Step-by-Step Study Skills

CERTIFICATE
OF
ACHIEVEMENT

THIS CERTIFICATE IS AWARDED TO

_____

IN RECOGNITION OF

_____

_____   _____

DATE   SIGNATURE

_____

TITLE

Made in the USA
Las Vegas, NV
07 September 2021

29775995R00039